Cracking
QUESTIONS

CW01497994

How to go beyond customer journey process mapping and really *improve the productivity of your business*

Questions and challenges that will help **you** *generate the dozen-plus small creative ideas that will enable your organisation* **to do more with less** *– and* **how to do this without** *the need to bring in large teams of costly 'transformation'* **consultants** *or use forests of flip chart paper 'mapping processes'.*

By Jon Harvey

First published in the United Kingdom in 2016 by
The Choir Press

ISBN 978-1-910864-31-9

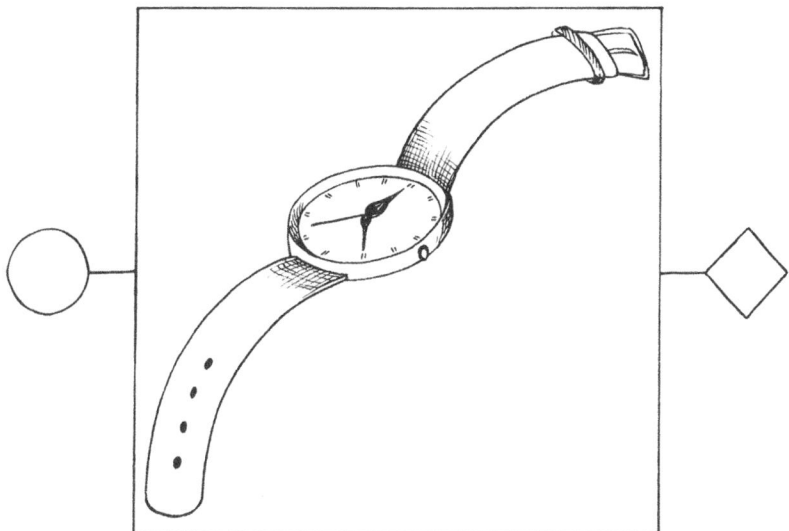

Introduction

You will be glad to know this is not a long book.

know how busy managers are: holding their teams together, tackling increasingly difficult performance challenges, making a profit and/or a difference ... and still trying to have a life outside work. And yes, I know: you have read many other business management books, earnestly hoping to find the ideas that will really help you deliver those results as a manager and leader. (And there are some really good books around. I have listed some at the end of this one.)

But still you are searching for those flashes of inspiration that will give you and your team (department/business/organisation ...) *the edge*. Everyone talks about the need to do more with less, but so often that seems in practice to be about working harder and harder but achieving less with less (whilst pretending it is more).

And you are told you can only get there if you pay for some expensive management consultants who, in time-honoured fashion, may well borrow your watch, tell you the time and keep the watch. They may also persuade you (not due to sharp practice but because they believe in it too) to spend hours, days, weeks even, 'mapping your business processes' as an essential basis for redesigning them to become 'lean'.

Every year, far too many organisations disappear down the rabbit hole of external management consultancy, some never to emerge again. But just as Alice didn't need anyone to tell her what to do, nor do you. You can climb *out* of the rabbit hole and go well beyond mere customer journey *mapping*.

This book is, in part, designed as the antidote to management consultants. And the author is (somewhat ironically) someone who has spent 26 years being a consultant. I am not saying that management consultants *never* add value. Why would I say that? No. But what I am saying is that 85% of what consultants are hired to do could be far, far better done by the people inside the organisation themselves.

This book is about helping you make the most of consultants when you absolutely need to use them. External consultants *can* illuminate, facilitate and even expurgate. But they should *never be hired to replicate* what is better done by those who know the organisation inside out.

So this short book is mainly about helping you and your colleagues do more *without* expensive consultants. The price of this book is roughly equivalent to just five minutes (or even less) of an expensive consultant's time. I think that makes this book a worthwhile bet if not a great long-term investment. I hope you do too.

What you will find in this book

- Why customer journey/process mapping is a waste of time
- What 'inductive' problem solving is all about and how you can apply it
- A few questions, carefully phrased, to help you redesign your processes and whole organisation (if you want to)
- Some examples to illustrate these questions and make them come alive
- Ideas on how to take all this forward with your team/organisation
- Appendices: other resources that can help

Some thanks

Even a book as slim as this one is never a solo project. I am hugely grateful to my two professional pals Paul Evans and Justin Willett; together we are the SpeakEasy Collective. Not only have they helped me to stay sane in recent years but they both provided invaluable feedback on an earlier draft. Suzette Davenport, a good client and friend, gave me some very useful insights from her perspective on an earlier version too. And a family friend, Katie Mossman, gave me some useful feedback. I am indebted to Mor Golan, who helped me reframe my thinking around how to invite people to read this book.

A heartfelt thank you to Miles Bailey and the whole team at the Choir Press, especially editor Harriet Evans and designer Adrian Sysum for their careful work on this book and for helping to bring it into being.

And this book would not have come about were it not for constant nudging from my dear brother, Kevin, and my wonderful son, Sam. Finally, without the sparkling love, tireless patience and fathomless support from my inspirational wife, Julie, very little would happen in my life.

This book is dedicated to my mother, who taught me how to ask good questions. What more could a son want or need?

The illustrations

I am also hugely grateful to my daughter, Jess Harvey, who has contributed in very many ways to the creation of the book you are reading. In particular, all the illustrations are hers. You can find more about her varied work at
http://www.jessharvey.com/

A promise

This book comes with my promise: if you do not find anything of value or use in this book, then please contact me and I will refund your money.

However, if the book helps you to find some ideas of great worth to you (as I hope and believe it will), please tell your friends and colleagues. And tell me too! I would love to hear your stories about how this book has helped create positive change.

Thanks.

Jon Harvey
Buckingham, UK

- jonharveyassociates.co.uk
- jonharveyassociates.blogspot.co.uk
- jon@jonharveyassociates.co.uk
- @jonsharvey

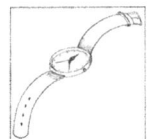

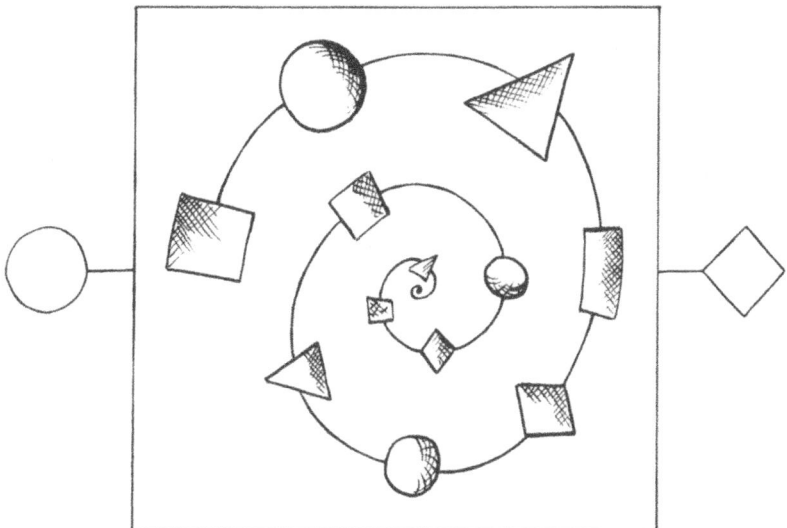

Why process mapping is a waste of time (and that includes customer journey mapping)

I believe that all you need to begin redesigning a process is a 'light map' which includes where/how the process starts and ends, with a few (probably no more than six) stages in between. This is enough to help you use the 'inductive problem solving' questions below.

But first let me tell you why I think many consultants will seek to persuade you to do lots and lots of process mapping (instead of my approach based on a light map):

- It is what they were taught to do and therefore it is what they believe you need to do as well.

- They are often technically or procedurally minded people with a computer programming background; mapping processes out in detail is just what they do.

- They believe that you need to know exactly, to a high level of detail, how things currently work in order to create a new shape for the future. You don't, in my view.

- Process mapping takes a lot of time and consumes large budgets of consultants' fees (or am I being just a tad *too* cynical here?).

- It looks very complicated and reinforces the notion that this is something that you could not possibly do without their help.

- It gives clients a warm secure feeling that they are getting something tangible for their money.

- Customer journey mapping often means you don't even have to involve real customers; you just pretend that you do by using the label.

And here is why I don't believe process mapping is worth the investment:

- It depletes the energy of the people involved in the process such that when the stage comes to redesigning the process creatively, there is nothing left in the tank and people are bored.

- No process map can capture just how things are really done. No matter how intricate the process map, real life is always more complex, idiosyncratic, contextual and therefore variable than a frozen image.

- It fixes people's attention on what is, rather than what could be.

- Process maps befuddle people and make them feel like cogs in a machine, whereas I believe that you actually want people to consider themselves to be (and indeed be) skilled actors in a play that they are helping to write.

- Because process mapping is and feels like a very technical approach, often only technical improvements emerge, whereas improvements can come from many different sources.

- Since so much effort is expended on process mapping, a range of small creative ideas are overlooked in the search for some single big fix that is proportionate to the effort.

In summary, only the lightest of 'mapping' is needed in order to find radical and transformational ways to deliver more with less. You can do this yourself without a) expensive process mapping software, b) expensive process mapping consultants and c) endless workshops to make sure the map is 'accurate', when it cannot ever be so anyway.

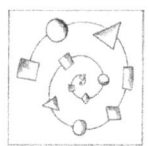

What 'inductive' problem solving is and how you can apply it

First, a quick recap on *deductive* problem solving. This involves a careful analysis of the current issue and then a suitably detailed set of investigations/experiments/statistics to work out the main causes of the problem. Solving the problem then becomes a task based on this analysis where the root causes are removed (or at least the effect of them is neutralised).

It is an essential method and one which forms the basis of most scientific endeavour as well as much organisational perform-ance improvement. It starts with the problem and works inwards, and then forwards to a new solution. *But it is not the only method . . .*

Inductive problem solving, on the other hand, starts with a solution and explores whether it might fit the problem in question. It is a more random approach and relies more on serendipity but is also often far more creative.

Take, for example, Edison's invention of the phonograph. It is reputed that when he came up with the invention, he was mostly focused on finding a way to record people's dying wishes and bequests. It took others to suggest the myriad of ways in which the basic idea could be adapted, including to the recording of music. In other words, Edison's solution was applied to many more problems or scenarios than he himself had ever considered.

Another famous example is of the 3M scientist who invented a glue that would not really stick. It took another 12 years before someone else happened upon the idea of Post-it notes, and the rest is history, as they say.

All the questions below have solutions embedded within them. Many of these embedded solutions will not fit the processes you are looking to improve. But several almost certainly will. If you ask the questions seriously, you may well find a solution for doing more with less that you will be frankly amazed you have not thought of before. Solutions for greater performance are often staring us in the face, sometimes for years! Or you may just find a few smaller improvements that could add up to make a big difference.

But I don't know.

But nor do you *until* you have asked the questions, carefully, openly and without any pre-set assumptions.

And in case you have not realised this yet: this does not have to be a lone activity. You can ask these questions and come up with inductive solutions in small groups and teams, and large multiple-stakeholder conventions. The chances are that there are several people you work with who have some excellent ideas about how to improve efficiency and effectiveness, both inside and outside your organisation, but for a variety of reasons they have not come forward with these ideas. Asking these questions in an engaging way may just provide the opportunity for them to do so. Moreover, magical things can happen when good conversations occur.

There are several effective ways to engage large and wider groups in this improvement activity. An Open Space process (see Appendix A) would be particularly effective at harnessing creativity, commitment and complexity in pursuit of ingenious solutions.

The 24 questions that will help you change the way business is done in your organisation

Further on is an explanation of each question, but here in one ready reckoner are some critical *process* redesign questions. (Later on there is a set of critical *service* redesign questions, aimed at helping you look at your overall organisation or business.)

1. Have we agreed the stakeholder requirements of the process?

2. Are those who run the process adequately trained?

3. Are there too many 'handovers'?

4. Is the process being done in the right order?

5. Could it be made simpler with a 'triage' stage?

6. Could we make better use of technology?

7. Where are the sources of rework?

8. Why does performance vary (and by how much)?

9. Could some parts of the process be done at the same time?

10. Are there too many checks and controls?

11. Could we get the users/clients/customers etc. to do more?

12. Could we get our partners/suppliers to take action?

13. Could different people or agencies be running the process (or part of it)?

14. Could we create an expert system to make it work more elegantly?

15. Is there a 'standard' way of carrying out the process?

16. Where are the delays or bottlenecks in the process?

17. Have we made any cultural or professional assumptions that are getting in the way?

18. Could we stop doing the process altogether?

19. Are decision-making protocols getting in the way?

20. Have we overlooked some well researched evidence-based practice?

21. Does the process contribute to our overall outcome goals?

22. Are we missing efficiency opportunities by not building in fail/stop gateways?

23. Have we listened to customer/client/user feedback enough?

24. What is really our 'bottom line' with this process?

These questions are not listed in any particular order. Indeed, I would recommend that you print out this list and create a set of cards to be picked from at random. The idea is simple:

- On your own, as a team/group or as a wider whole system or network of people, focus on the process needing to be redesigned, with the 'light map' in view.

- Pose each of these questions carefully, but exploratively . . .

- Then see what happens; the discussion can follow.

- Allow for plenty of silence while people think, use their imagination or reconcile themselves to very different ways of working.

And that is it.

I could *try* to make the process more complicated, write a few more chapters and so forth. But would that help you?

Meanwhile, here are some more explanations and stories behind each question.

The questions unpacked

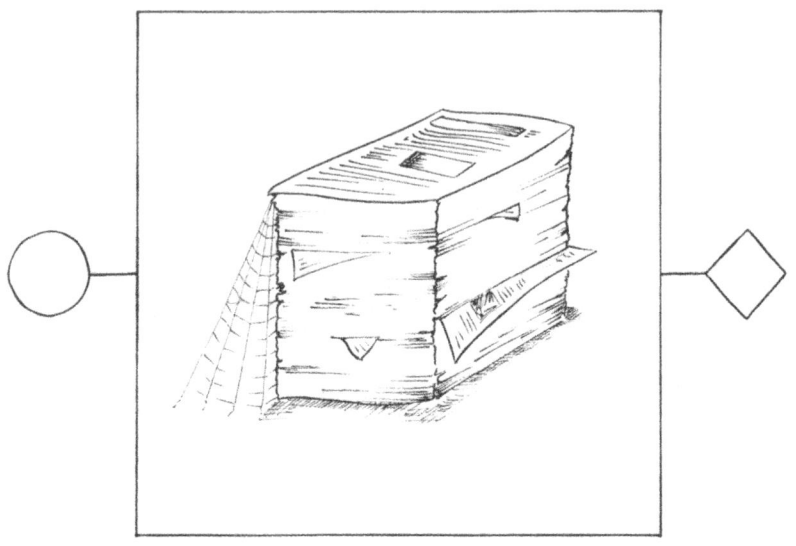

1. Have we agreed the stakeholder requirements of the process?

I was working with the management team of a manufacturing company once. The discussion happened upon reviewing a monthly report produced by the engineering director. He explained that it took him two days each month to analyse the data and produce the report. I asked the rest of the team how they used the report in their parts of the business. They all looked blank and a little sheepish. It turned out that while a couple glanced at the report, nobody really used it to help build or even simply run the business.

But then something more interesting happened. The discussion turned into a debate about what analysis *would* be useful, and the engineering director left with a new specification for a monthly report that was going to take him less time to produce but which would be read and used productively by the rest of the team.

All processes are likely to have been right at least once (optimally efficient, effective, useful). But the people involved with running the process, receiving the outputs from the process, providing inputs to the process and benefiting from the outcomes of the process ... change. What matters to them changes. Their requirements change. The world changes.

So this question is about all that: who are the stakeholders in the process, and have their requirements of the process been *agreed recently*? They need to be *agreed* because it is a two-way street and *recently* because things change.

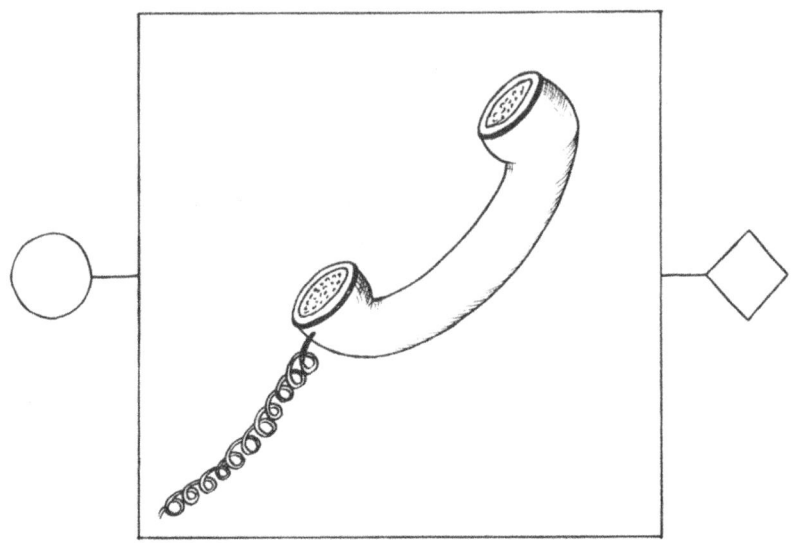

2. Are those who run the process adequately trained?

Not long ago, I was sent a random email out of the blue asking me if I wanted some new business cards printed. As it happened, I was in the market. I liked the friendly tone of this cold-calling email and replied. A few days later (not a good sign), I received an email back which raised a couple of questions in my mind. One of these questions related to where the company was based. I phoned the number at the bottom of the email and a woman picked up. She appeared to know nothing about the firm, including where it was based. All she was empowered/trained to do was take a message. I ordered my new business cards from someone else.

This is just one example of the myriad of issues that can be uncovered with this question. If the staff employed to run a process are not given sufficient training, development, mentoring, coaching, instruction, information, it is more than likely that the process is not running at optimum efficiency and effectiveness.

I know this is an obvious question! But how many miserable, frustrated and even angry employees, customers and suppliers have you come across in your time because this basic question has not been properly addressed? And addressed not just once, but on a regular basis. This is a critical management activity.

3. Are there too many 'handovers'?

From a customer's perspective, the classic example of this is when we phone up our bank, energy provider or council and get passed from pillar to post; each time, we have to give the same information over and over and over again. But inside organisations, it is far worse than this.

A handover is when responsibility for running a process shifts from one individual or department or team etc. to another. Information, insights, materials, products etc. are handed over from one to another. And when this happens, something always gets lost in transit. This loss invariably needs to be made up in some way, which only creates inefficiency and ineffectiveness, and frustration!

A couple of handovers in a process is not a huge problem, but when they start numbering four, five or even ten-plus, with some piece of information or object being passed back and forth, the process gets seriously unstable. The redesign answer to this is to appoint a case manager who, whilst consulting key people along the way, retains overall control and knowledge of what is happening to the service/case/product. Indeed, having a case manager allows the process to happen in a more rounded way than in a purely linear fashion, which does not always fit.

So if you have a process where the marketeers, designers, makers, producers, sellers and frontline providers (or whatever you call them in your business) often fall out with each other, this could be a question well worth investigating.

4. Is the process being done in the right order?

I was once doing a small piece of work with some traffic engineers working for a local council in the north of England. They explained to me how they went about resolving the issue of whether to install road humps in a residential street in order to slow traffic down. Stage A was that they received a letter from a member of the public requesting such humps. Stage B was to explore all the perspectives, talk with local councillors, and survey the street with theodolites and the like. Stage C was to prepare a committee report on the viability and usefulness of such a scheme. Stage D, subject to the will of the councillors, was to consult the rest of the street. Stage E was to install the road humps. However, sometimes at stage D they found out good reasons from other local residents as to why not to install road humps or indeed found out that the rest of the street's residents were vehemently opposed to the idea. If that were the case, the work would be stopped. I asked them why they did not do stage D earlier in the process and possibly save themselves a whole heap of redundant work (stage C, for example). With their engineers' heads on, they looked at me with their heads tipped to one side. But with their public managers' heads on they could see where I was coming from.

So in the processes that you look after, are there stages which, if done earlier (or later or in a different order entirely), would make the process that much more fit for purpose? The purpose of a process is to achieve something, not just do something.

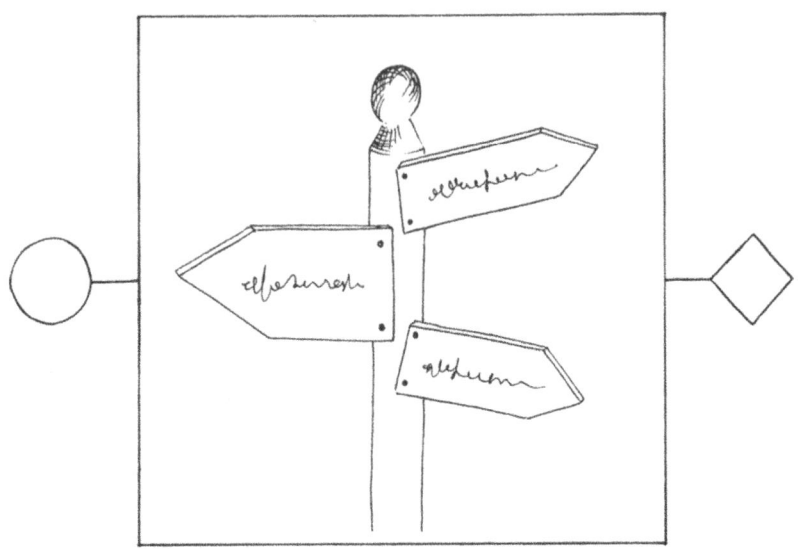

5. Could it be made simpler with a 'triage' stage?

Often for very good reasons (although also often not), processes end up becoming a rather complex set of loops with rather intricate technical stages. This could be due to past quality failures, the need to comply with externally imposed regulations or just because it was the right course to follow at the time in certain instances. However, it takes many resources to put every case down this complicated route. And with many cases, it does not have to be that complicated.

Take for example the process of appointing a new headteacher for a school, which is a process requiring proper scrutiny of the applicants and their career histories, consultation with various stakeholder groups (such as parents, students and local officials), and the creation of a rigorous assessment process. The process is complicated but absolutely appropriately so. However, if that same school were to appoint a new (say) French assistant, the process would not need to be as onerous. What has happened here is that a triage stage has been installed at the front end of the process to determine which route the new case should go down: the complicated one, the slightly less complicated one or the fast track one (say).

Thus a carefully designed triage stage (and there can be more than one) can channel cases down process routes that need fewer resources and can be completed much more quickly. The art in installing such a redesign is making the triage stage(s) workable and fit for purpose.

We use triage every day, but sometimes we forget to use the concept in processes that we work with every day.

6. Could we make better use of technology?

The answer to this question is almost always 'yes', of course. And there will be a queue of software and hardware suppliers standing outside your door in nanoseconds once you admit to this answer. However, it then becomes much more complicated and buckets of money are thrown at ever-expanding IT project teams as they discover even more bells and whistles to add to the growing system being created. Almost inevitably, the system being designed, like a one-way spaceship, drifts further and further away from the Earth.

I exaggerate, of course, and some of my best friends are systems geeks ... but there is an inherent problem here, if it can be spotted. The answer beyond 'yes' can become one that is disproportionately technology-led rather than suitably outcome-led. I add the qualifications to make the point that innovation *can* come from the 'what if' questions that new technology can provoke. But focusing on the technology over the outcome can also mean that the 'solution' is just not a solution.

The art of addressing this question comes from choosing to exploit the *minimum* of technology. One example of this comes from a piece of work I did with some staff from a youth offending team (YOT), which seeks to enable young people to turn away from a life of crime. One of the principal methods of doing this is using restorative justice, where offenders are confronted with their victims and learn about the impact of their offending on the victims' lives. As you might expect, many of the YOT's clients had got mixed up in shoplifting, which is not the victimless crime that they sometimes thought it was. Ideally, the young offenders should learn about the consequences of their crime from a live manager of the shop that they stole from. But, of course, those managers could not be made to leave their work every time a young person needed to hear this message. So the solution that emerged was to film a range of managers explaining to camera what happened when shoplifting occurred. The young clients of the YOT could then be shown this film at a later date. Not as powerful as a real live person, but better than nothing.

This was a low-technology solution that helped improve the service. Not all technology needs to be cutting-edge to create productive improvements.

In Appendix A there is a special subset of questions that can be posed to support this overall one in order to stimulate creative inductive problem solving.

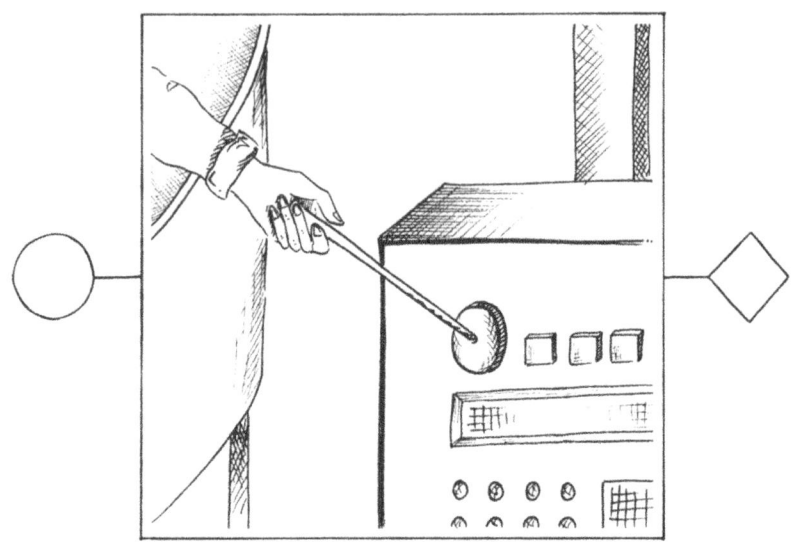

7. Where are the sources of rework?

Over many years in many organisations, I have observed some remarkably high levels of comfort with processes going wrong and with the resulting effort to correct the presenting surface problems. However, the time needed to focus on *why* the process keeps going wrong is often seen as impossible to find, whereas the time needed to carry out the rework resulting from the failed process always seems to be found.

This is a particular passion of mine. A while ago I uploaded a video (in two parts) explaining how this problem comes about and what should be done about it. I have put the links to the video in Appendix A. It is about how 'quick-fix' approaches to problem solving need to be replaced by 'stay-fix' approaches.

Understanding what parts of a process regularly need to be reworked is key to redesigning that process. These are the flashing red warning arrows on a process pointing towards where you need to take robust preventative action. This question forces you to look for these places.

I remember hearing the story of a large manufacturing machine operator who spent a considerable portion of his shift going from one level of his machine to another to fix a problem that kept reoccurring. He had done this for years, reducing the productivity on his machine significantly.

I was told the story by a trade union rep who once spent a night shift observing this operator's night-time equivalent tackling this problem. This night shift worker had discovered (or perhaps had read in the instruction manual!) that there was a specially designed piece of equipment: a long stick, more or less. This enabled the machine to be reset easily and quickly when the same problem occurred.

The trade union rep went back and showed the day shift worker, who had seen the stick but never used it, just what it was for. The rep told me that the look of anguish on his face was almost too hard to watch. Sometimes the realisation that there is a simpler way of performing a task can be painful.

Notwithstanding the need to recognise and manage the emotions that are caught up in causing the rework, it is vital to keep focused on making the process work better.

8. Why does performance vary (and by how much)?

Everything varies; you only have to look at nature to know that variation and diversity are what makes the world such a beautiful place.

Even though there are people in every organisation who earnestly wish that processes did not vary, the process performance will, nonetheless, go up and down. The art of good process management (and redesign) is understanding where and when the performance varies and then taking subtle and informed action to reduce this variation progressively.

There are many good books on statistical process control (SPC) and two are referenced in Appendix A. In essence SPC and process management are all about distinguishing between the variations in performance which should be responded to and the variations which should not be.

For example, if a die is thrown repeatedly, some patterns of results reveal a perfectly balanced die where the six numbers are rolled with more or less equal frequency, while others would indicate a loaded one, showing one number coming up far more often than others. Knowing what patterns of random variations can be expected and what patterns are not provides the basis for improving the performance of any process.

Every school wants its students there on time every school day, ready and willing to learn. Unsurprisingly schools put huge efforts into ensuring that parents get their children to school on time, and many regularly send letters home reminding parents of their responsibility to ensure this happens. In one school I worked with, we analysed the performance data on school attendance. We found that letters home made not one jot of difference; the data proved it. However, what did make the difference on many days was the weather. Rain encouraged more parents to drive their children to school, the roads became clogged with more cars and it was the consequent delays that resulted in negative performance trends on school attendance.

And so the redesigned process focused on advising parents to share transport on wet mornings or get their offspring good raincoats!

9. Could some parts of the process be done at the same time?

When I worked with the Consumers' Association many years ago, they were facing the problem that when they published the reports on 'best buys' in their magazine *Which?*, the products were often no longer on the shelves. The research process had become so long that it was exceeding the shelf life of those products. So when you went to purchase the best buy 'Zuperissimo ZX451TL' dishwasher, that model was no longer available. Their solution was not to cut the research process but to parallel drive it instead. Parts of the process that had hitherto been carried out in sequence were carried out at the same time, while adequate communication loops were installed to ensure that overall coherence of the process was not lost.

It is the process redesign equivalent of boiling your potatoes at the same time as the roast is cooking in the oven. It is also the essence of good project management.

10. Are there too many checks and controls?

remember once walking into the office of a shop floor manager and noticing a box holding the door open, containing what looked to be stacks of computer printouts. I asked the manager what they were. He explained they were the performance monitoring reports on various parts of the production process. I raised my eyebrows quizzically and he said, 'Yep, they are good for holding the door open.'

I use this example to illustrate that whilst huge efforts go into creating detailed structures that are concerned with checking and controlling processes, very often the data is never used and can be a distraction from the real business. Unless the information emerging from a check or control is used, it is just an expensive overhead. It is like the old saying: weighing a pig does not make it any heavier.

We live in highly litigious and 'back-protecting' days where such checks and controls are used like a drunk uses a lamppost: not for illumination but for support. But it does not have to be this way. This question is designed to prompt an investigation into whether there are any checks, controls or other performance measures (especially ones that consume large amounts of time and resources) that are known to be redundant. If there are, take action to design them out of the system. Often there are ways to build these controls into the process itself so that it is self-controlling. IT can help, or even just well-designed checklists.

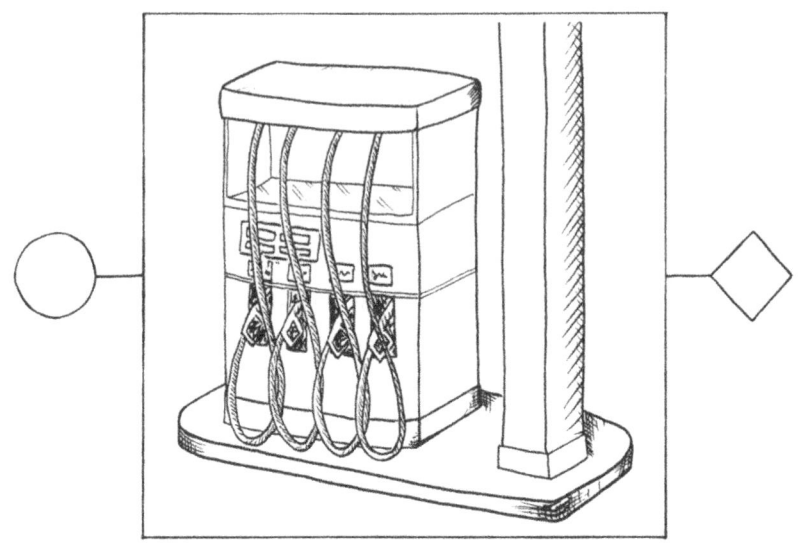

11. Could we get the users/clients/ customers etc. to do more?

When we wander around supermarkets, especially the ones laid out on exposed metal racking, are we not just unpaid warehouse staff? When we fill up our fuel tanks at petrol stations, are we not just doing the work of now long-forgotten forecourt attendants, who would clean your windscreen too? As we use self-checkouts, internet shopping malls, blood pressure monitors ... etc.

The commercial and public service world is now filled with examples of jobs being done by users/clients/customers that had previously been done for them. I am sure you can think of many more. This question is all about whether we have gone as far as we can. Is there more we can do to engage the service receivers, not only to improve efficiency but also to make it a better and more empowering experience for them?

Imagine for example that your house has been burgled and you phone the police. Let us also imagine that they say they will be round later on to 'dust the scene', as it were. You are probably feeling defiled, angry, upset and a whole heap of other emotions, including a sense of powerlessness. The police have a choice: to leave you to wait with all those emotions or ask you to take action yourself. They could ask, for example, for you to make a list of all the items that appear to have been moved. This might flag up places from where fingerprints could be lifted. Which option would be better for you and for them? Which might help their investigations and perhaps even the recovery of the items you have lost, not to mention the arrest of the person involved? And which might help to make you feel back in control?

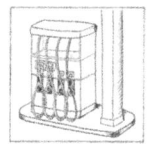

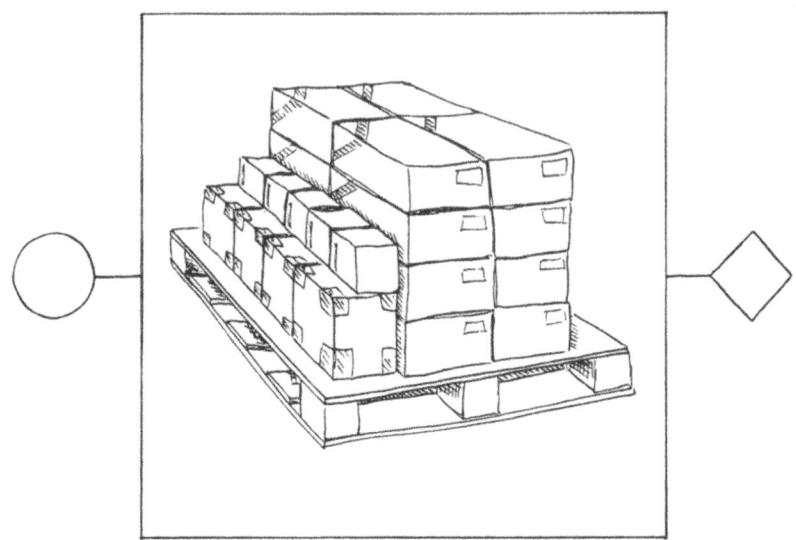

12. Could we get our partners/suppliers to take action?

Of course, sharing the workload of a process and making it more streamlined is not just about engaging the customers more. It can also be about examining whether the supplies to your processes could be improved. The suppliers might be at the 'head' of your process or be partners along the route who provide logistical support or advice (so-called secondary suppliers).

This can boil down to being more precise about your requirements, adopting a *kanban* approach whereby supplies are only drawn down as required by the manufacturing producers. Or this can be by ensuring that the state in which supplies arrive at the 'door' of the process helps to speed it up, not slow it down. This might include holding suppliers to account for the quality of the supplies they provide to you, whether information or materials, such that you do not have to carry out a quality check. You just assume the specification is as required.

Tight agreed procedures and shared trust are what makes process redesigns based on this question viable. Indeed, the investigations leading from this question may well lead to some answers to the question below. If you are doing your suppliers' work for them, perhaps they should be doing it. Moreover, it might be better business for you *and* them if you outsource the process (or part of the process) to them.

There can be small improvements made based on this question, such as the corner shop that requests the delivery pallets are stacked in a different order, which makes little difference to the supplier but a huge difference to the shop owner. Or it can lead you and your suppliers down the quality assurance (QA) route of ISO 9000 (or BS 5750, as it used to be, which began life as AQAP: the NATO supplier QA system). It can also extend into using whole system methods (see Appendix A for more information) to bring together partners in big conversations about achieving strategic outcomes together with greater understanding and joint action.

It is a simple question with a wide range of possible answers.

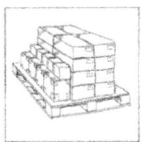

13. Could different people
or agencies be
running the process
(or part of it)?

Sometimes when you come to examine a process and think boldly and creatively about it, you realise that your organisation is simply not best placed to run this process. The risks of handing a process over to another body are, of course, significant and the outcomes into a distant future uncertain. So proper due diligence is needed, naturally, before making this choice. But in a world where resources continue to be very tight, such choices need to be considered.

Much of this has been happening for many years. We have seen a fragmentation and privatisation of many government services with a wide variety of results, some not especially positive. Whilst many big businesses still want to grow through merger and acquisition, many other companies now exist as virtual networks of smaller businesses and freelance suppliers. Though controversial (mainly for its low rates of pay), Amazon's Mechanical Turk is a busy marketplace for disassembled processes.

There is a growing interest in how big the so-called 'sharing economy', where people hire out resources that they are currently underutilising, is set to grow. This can include rooms in people's homes (Airbnb) or cars (Uber). It is not a new idea; neighbours have been sharing tools across the fence for many centuries. But technology is opening up new possibilities. Is this one of the answers to this question?

14. Could we create an expert system to make it work more elegantly?

One of the great earners for some management consultancies and IT companies in recent years has been knowledge management (KM). Lew Platt, the former CEO of Hewlett-Packard, said one day, 'If only HP knew what HP knows, we would be three times more productive.' This is one of the prompts that started a whole industry in KM.

This is not the place to indulge in a critique of the value of KM strategies. But this question does highlight the importance of knowledge in determining the elegant flow of some processes.

Of course the phrase 'expert system' conjures up some kind of scary artificial intelligence where a myriad of responses to a predicted set of parameters are coded and put inside a box with blinking eyes. But it does not have to be that way. An expert system can simply be the small checklist of things to remember when carrying out a specific task. It can be a set of people to call in certain prescribed circumstances, also known as a 'phone a friend' list; that too is an expert system. An expert system can be an instruction manual that came with the machine. The system needs to be proportionate to the process in hand.

Some years ago I was working with senior managers from a single organisation, who were spread out across the country. They were all wrestling with a set of broadly common problems. So, as part of some leadership development workshops I was facilitating for them, we gradually compiled a list of 'cunning wheezes' that they had each separately discovered/worked out/created to tackle their common challenges. I organised the list a little and gave it back to them. This became their expert system.

15. Is there a 'standard' way of carrying out the process?

Of course one of the usual ways of creating an expert system is to turn the blend of custom and practice, ambitions and existing process instructions into a tight quality standard. In many industries these standards are essential not least for quality compliance, but also for business success and the health and wellbeing of staff and customers.

For many other organisations, the effort to create such regimented standards is seen as disproportionately onerous and not cost-effective. Indeed, even the ones who have committed to creating such standards may well feel the same.

But the standard way does not have to be to a weighty tome of procedural instructions. I once visited a hospital ward where the standards were illustrated as sets of photographs. As we all know, a picture tells a thousand words. And so it was with these pictures.

Indeed, with the availability of easy filming and uploading to the likes of YouTube, it is possible to create standards in ways that are far less onerous and far more helpful. For example, on the net now are video instructions for how to do all manner of DIY tasks around the house. And so on.

16. Where are the delays or bottlenecks in the process?

read a book many years ago entitled *The Goal*, by Eliyahu M Goldratt and Jeff Cox. It is written in the form of a novel about someone learning some key insights into manufacturing. I recommend it to you. One of the insights is the critical need to avoid bottlenecks as these invariably increase costs and are indicators of something going very wrong with a process.

So this question is all about identifying any delays in a process and examining the root causes of these delays. A good approach to doing this is to ask the six honest men of Rudyard Kipling:

I keep six honest serving-men
(They taught me all I knew);
Their names are What and Why and When,
And How and Where and Who

I remember hearing a story about a manufacturing machine that kept shutting down for no apparent reason and causing severe bottlenecks. Delays invariably ensured as it was recalibrated and started once more. These delays were costing a great deal of money and no single engineer had managed to work out the cause. A quality problem-solving group was given the task to dig deeper. As part of their investigation, they bashed all six questions around a bit. It was when they asked the 'when' question that lightbulbs suddenly came on, almost literally. On certain days when it was bright and at a certain time, the sunlight came around the edge of the building and shone through the window onto the machine in question. It heated up and stopped working properly. This was a pattern that no one had seen until then.

17. Have we made any cultural or professional assumptions that are getting in the way?

It is very hard to see the assumptions we make, since they are often invisible to us. It usually takes someone else to point them out. This is where customers/suppliers/users/citizens have a particularly important role to play. Their angle is a very different one and they can often see the elephant in the room that people on the inside simply cannot see.

But what assumptions might these be?

I came across a very clear example from a local council once: they had been looking at the process they used to repair faulty street lamps. Hitherto, if a member of the public phoned in and explained the street light outside their house wasn't working, the council would despatch an engineer to see if the street light was, indeed, not working. Invariably they found out that it wasn't, so then a second engineer was sent to fix it.

On creative examination of what they were doing, they realised they could halve the process by simply believing the members of the public who phoned in. In other words, they were making the assumption that people who reported street lamps as not working could be malevolent troublemakers and out to waste precious public resources. But when they realised that, in all likelihood, this was not the case, they could change their process dramatically.

There was a time when dropped kerbs were something of a rarity. Now they are much more common, although still absent in some critical places. The cultural assumption that was made was that only people in wheelchairs needed such dropped kerbs and there aren't that many of 'them'. People challenged this assumption partly on the basis of human rights, but also on the basis that many more people would benefit from such changes.

I am not sure I could verify this, but I have a hunch that the industry of suitcases and briefcases on wheels, as well as the proliferation of electric scooters for people with mobility impairments, would not have grown so much without a change in this cultural assumption.

Challenging core assumptions can provoke a great deal of resistance. This means that the *way* in which these assumptions are uncovered and questioned is critical to success. A carefully designed intervention or meeting is required.

18. Could we stop doing the process altogether?

It is a simple question. It is the case that sometimes things are done that were once important and useful, but times change. And in that moving on, someone somewhere forgot to stop the process that relied on the old regime or market conditions (etc.) for its value. So it might seem like a daft question, but it is often answered 'yes'.

I have seen people look crestfallen when they are told, because they asked this question, that their 'monthly report' which takes several days to produce is read by no one. If asked and answered carefully, this question has the potential to liberate businesses and people from grinding processes that add no value.

How many business cards or websites have you seen recently that feature fax numbers . . . ?

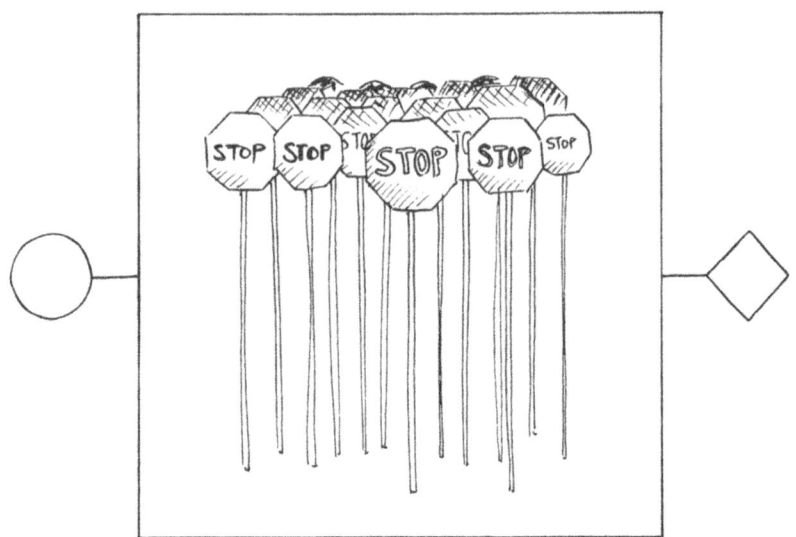

19. Are decision-making protocols getting in the way?

Some years ago, I came across an intriguing model called 'responsibility charting' in a book; in fact it was the first ever book on organisational development that I read. The book was *Organizational Transitions: Managing Complex Change* by Richard Beckhard and Reuben T Harris (Addison-Wesley, 1977). The model proposes that in any decision, there is a selection of roles present: the person(s) responsible for initiating action to ensure that the decision is carried out (ideally only one person has this role); person(s) from whom approval must be sought and who accordingly have a right of veto; persons who provide logistical support, advice, information or resources, and those who must be informed but cannot influence the decision. And there are some who are not involved at all. It is a helpful model as it can expose just how full of unnecessary ballast many managerial or process decisions are.

In one charity I worked with once, we carried out some responsibility charting. Invariably we found process decisions handicapped both by confusion as to who should be initiating the decisions and by the large numbers of people having to be consulted for their approval/veto. Everything was grinding to a halt. Often!

So this question asks you to look candidly, frankly and honestly at how critical decisions are made. You might be surprised by the results.

20. Have we overlooked some well researched evidence-based practice?

Custom and practice build up over many years in organisations. You would expect that with all that experience and testing, the best practice would always emerge. It can, but only if the organisation is committed to people reflecting on what they do, conducting a proportionate amount of experimentation, keeping up to date with good practice elsewhere and so on. However, many organisations don't do this and their practices can become frozen in time, immune to better practice elsewhere.

So this question is designed to get people to look outside, examine the research and benchmark practice against other organisations which are doing better. These other organisations do not even need to be in the same business.

A classic example of this is Southwest Airlines, who are credited with a significant benchmarking study. This airline, one of the first 'cheap' airlines, reasoned that when a plane is in the air it is earning money. When it is on the ground, it is not. So they decided to find out how they could turn their aircraft around more quickly from one arrival to the next departure. At this point, they sought the assistance of a Formula One racing team and, with their help, unpacked and dissected what happened in a pit stop. They then took this learning back to their own business and made some rapid improvements in turnaround time.

21. Does the process contribute to our overall outcome goals?

There is a great book, *Will It Make the Boat Go Faster? Olympic-Winning Strategies for Everyday Success* (by Ben Hunt-Davis and Harriet Beveridge, 2011), which is all about focusing on clear outcomes and learning as you go. In other words, if you are doing something that isn't making the boat go faster, then stop doing it or change it so it is.

So whatever your outcome goals are, this question challenges you to say how a process is helping to achieve them. If you cannot say it in simple straightforward language, something probably needs to change.

And of course, you do need to be clear on what your outcome goals are (more customers who recommend you, less fear of crime, more return on investment, greater profit etc). This isn't always an easy question to answer or find agreement on. Try asking four colleagues and see if their answers diverge or converge.

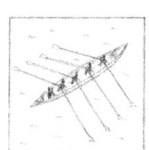

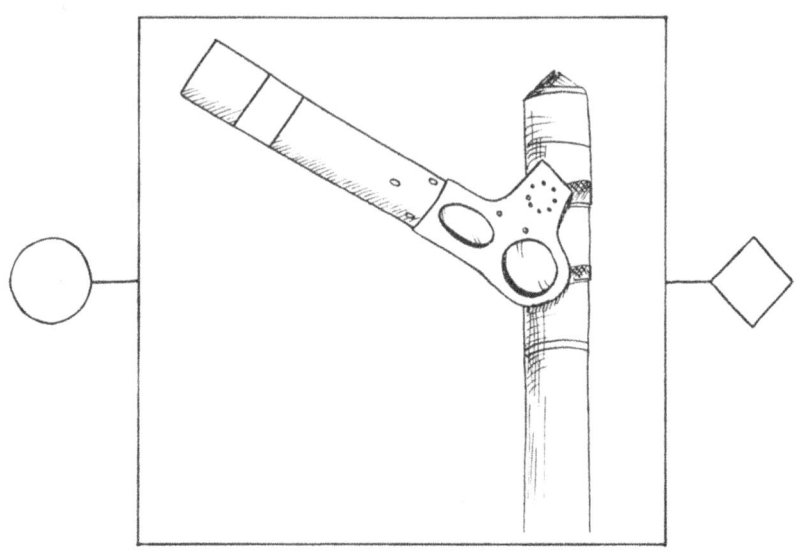

22. Are we missing efficiency opportunities by not building in fail/stop gateways?

*P*oka-yoke is the Japanese term for mistake-proofing a process. It is the quality equivalent of failsafe. And we all know about these systems now; we order articles online. How many times has a screen frozen and pointed out to us that we have failed to give some necessary piece of information? This is building in fail/stop gateways.

Many process stages rely upon the previous stage being correct. This question simply asks whether such measures are built into the system or not. If not, the chances are that human error will intervene and the mistake requiring rework will be discovered at some later point. Indeed, by that point, it might be quite hard to work out where the mistake happened in the first place in anything more than the simplest processes.

As a town councillor, I am often reviewing planning applications. Although my council is not the final decision maker (the local bigger district council is), our view is very much taken into account. However, it is not uncommon for an application to come to our planning committee missing several important pieces of information (such as site plan) or with the information only having been uploaded a day or two before. If I had my way, the clock would not start ticking on a planning application (the district council must respond within a set time period) until *all* the requisite documents had been submitted. This would, I wish, be one example of an improved process that not only put the onus on the applicant to get everything correct from the outset but would also ensure a reliable gateway on which to base the rest of the application process.

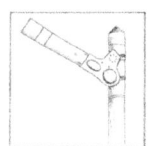

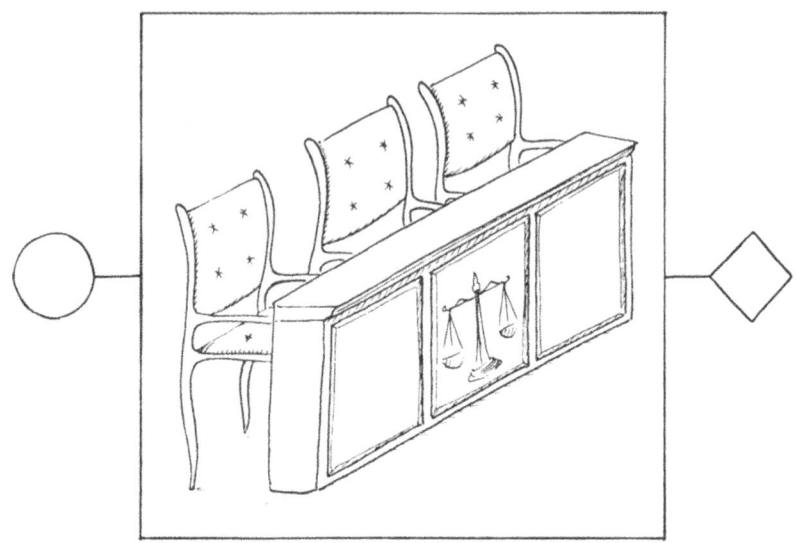

23. Have we listened to customer/client/user feedback enough?

More than 25 years ago, I began my consultancy career in the field of total quality management. Back then, the concept of building your business around what the customers wanted and needed was an innovation. Sadly, in all too many companies and organisations . . . it still is. In so many companies, shiny posters, Twitter feeds, feedback surveys and legions of market researchers are merely evidence of the *lip service* paid to concept of listening to customers, but the reality is still some way off.

Any review of a business process must begin with asking what our customers/clients/users are saying. What works for them, what doesn't work for them? How can we jiggle, shuffle, twist and refine the process so that it addresses what they are saying to us and comes closer to what they want and need? Many new business ventures have risen out of older, established ones when they have asked this question. Indeed, customers are often one of the richest sources of innovation and improvement.

And it doesn't have to be a big, statistically balanced sample; just one person's feedback can make a difference, if you want it to. I well remember one person saying to me that there are no allocated seats in a courtroom for the family of a murdered victim. There are seats for the judge, for the jury, lawyers, press and accused, of course, and for the general public. But nowhere special for the people whom the crime has most affected. This is still a change I am waiting to see happen in the 'victim-centric' courts service.

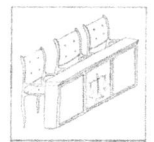

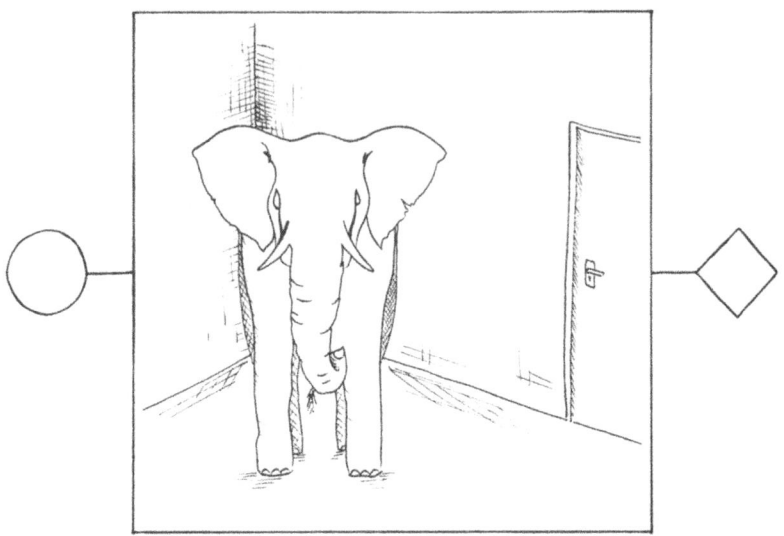

24. What is really our
'bottom line' with this
process?

Sometimes, there are features of how an organisation carries out its business that everyone knows, but probably won't admit in public, are deeply inefficient and perhaps even profoundly ineffective. However, these methods are allowed to continue due to some historic glitch, some other overriding commitment or perhaps a family matter which has become irrevocably mixed up with business. You probably know the kind of thing I am talking about.

I remember working with one organisation once, where one of the directors had a close familial relationship with one of the company owners. 95% of what this director did added no value to the company whatsoever. Talking about any of this was deemed hugely risky and therefore everyone ignored this 'elephant in the room'. The company went bust a year or two later, my observations having been ignored.

So this question dares to uncover such possibilities. It may be 'career-limiting' to do so or it may not be. It is a tough call. Sometimes external advisers are brought in to be honest and courageous, and ask such questions.

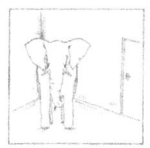

The 11 questions that will help you decide whether process redesign is enough

When looking to improve what an organisation achieves, merely redesigning the processes may not be enough. Sometimes what is required is a radical transformation of the whole service/business/company. These questions are designed to help you decide how far you need to go.

Question	Rating	Score
1. How much external pressure to redesign the service is there?	Not much (1) to We really have no choice (5)	
2. Past restructures/redesigned services have proved to be very beneficial.	Disagree a lot (1) to Agree a lot (5)	
3. Redesigning the service is the only option available to us.	Disagree a lot (1) to Agree a lot (5)	
4. What are the chances that a redesign of the service would lead to significant improvements?	Low (1) to High (5)	
5. How high are key stakeholder expectations that we should redesign the service?	Low (1) to High (5)	
6. We have already tried a number of improvement activities with little effect.	Disagree a lot (1) to Agree a lot (5)	
7. How recent was the last redesign of the service?	Very recent (1) to Never happened before (5)	
8. The time is now ripe for a redesign of the service.	Disagree a lot (1) to Agree a lot (5)	
9. Redesigning the service would help reshape and release staff talents.	Disagree a lot (1) to Agree a lot (5)	
10. The benefits arising out of a redesign of the service would outweigh the costs.	Disagree a lot (1) to Agree a lot (5)	
11. The service processes are so intricately linked that a process redesign would not work well.	Disagree a lot (1) to Agree a lot (5)	
Total (out of maximum of 55)		

The higher the score, the greater the chance that a redesign of the whole service would be more beneficial than just a few process redesigns.

The 20 questions that will help you lead service redesign and business transformation

These are questions from a *whole* organisation viewpoint, not just looking at one of the processes. You will see that many of the questions are similar to the 24 process questions from before, but tweaked to apply to a whole service.

1. Have we established what outcomes our citizens/customers/clients want and need this year, and is our business shaped around them?

2. Have we agreed other stakeholder requirements for objectives, outcomes and outputs?

3. Does our service join up with other services and businesses in a way that fits with the 'joined up' lives of the people we serve?

4. Is the service/business designed around old thinking/technology/practice?

5. Where are the sources of frustration with the service for the people we serve? Why might people be voting with their feet?

6. Could this service/business be 'piggy-backed' onto another?

7. What would happen if we stopped providing this service/doing this business? What would fill the vacuum?

8. Could we commission our partners or suppliers to deliver this service/business?

9. Could we commission community-based organisations/others to deliver this service?

10. Could we commission customers/clients etc. to 'deliver' this service to themselves?

11. Does our organisational culture need redesigning rather than the service? If so, how?

12. Have we made any cultural or professional assumptions that are getting in our way?

13. Are the performance objectives or measures helping to deliver outcomes?

14. Does the service have too many or too few resources?

15. Does the business model work (really)?

16. Have we got the right lines of ownership/accountability/governance arrangements in place?

17. Would the service/business benefit from co-location with another (in reality or virtually with knowledge/information)?

18. Are there any hard legacy architectures (finance, IT, HR, legal, estate etc.) that need to be worked around?

19. Are there any partnership arrangements or requirements that open up or close down whole service/business redesign possibilities?

20. Is a service redesign better than a process redesign? Why or why not?

Many of these questions will not apply to your organisation, but perhaps one or two of them will. As before, they are designed to help you see your business from a different angle. And, also as before, the more inclusively you can address these questions (by engaging staff, suppliers, customers, funders, regulators, perhaps even market competitors), the more likely it is that you will arrive at some helpful answers. Not only will these answers shake up old ways of doing business, but in amongst those new ways could be the one that will lead to greater success.

It all depends on how bold you want to be. And that depends on how much you want or need to change. If you are content with how your organisation/service/business is structured, then do not ask yourself any of these questions.

If you are not content, ask them well, and search deeply and creatively for the answers.

Taking these ideas forward: the 11 challenges to address

It is one matter to come up with ideas. It is quite another to make those ideas happen. There is a whole other book on leading such change successfully; indeed, many books have been written on this subject.

But it would not be right to produce a book like this and not give at least some pointers on how to prepare the ground before the questions above are even asked. It is also helpful to make some suggestions on how to turn the emerging ideas into robust everyday practice.

As with the rest of the book, I will aim to be succinct.

Firstly, it is wise to be aware of the challenges facing you when you embark on transforming processes or whole businesses. Here are some of them:

1. *Communication.* If I had hot dinners for the number of organisations I have been in to that have said they have a problem with communication . . . yada yada! Again, a whole other book, if not several, could be and has been written on this. But suffice to say that rumours and misconceptions about service and process transformation can suck out the life of a transformation initiative. Social media and instant communication via email (etc.) have only served to make rumours even easier to spread. This needs managing.

2. *Concern over job or role loss.* People will naturally be worried, and why should turkeys vote for Christmas by offering insights into how processes might be done

better? This can only be handled with carefully constructed HR and redundancy policies so that everyone knows where they stand. Any perceived lack of honesty and transparency will not work in your favour. Trust is a critical ingredient here.

3. *IT . . . the myth and the reality.* Beware of promises that IT can make real all your process and service redesign dreams. It cannot. Watch out for snake oil transformation consultants who will try to sell you castles in the air. IT is there to serve transformation, not shape it.

4. *Need for investment for IT skills/knowledge.* IT can and does make huge differences, of course. But when you purchase the hardware and software, don't forget to buy the upgrading of the people who will be operating the new systems as well. How many carefully designed and installed functions are simply overlooked because no one spent the time telling the users about them and, more importantly, how to use these functions?

5. *Prioritisation.* Many companies floundered and/or foundered with business process reengineering (BPR) because they simply bit off more than they could chew. Rather than pleasing the customer, many businesses ended up feeding the BPR consultants instead. Prioritising is critical and it takes a chunk of time. But this time is well spent if it yields the plan that targets the six critical processes up for redesign rather than the 66 processes that must all be changed in the next three weeks.

6. *Involvement of service users/customers/citizens.* It is only natural that most organisations suffer from varying degrees of introspection. Customers represent a different tribe, and they can be an awkward lot. However, these are the people whose support keeps you in business and, strangely, they can be very loyal! As mentioned above, these external people see what you do from a very different perspective. If you fail to engage them, you will lose not only their potential creativity but also, more worryingly, their support as you leave them behind.

7. *Appropriateness of the techniques.* There is something of a fashion for importing ideas, structures and values from one kind of organisation to another. This can work or it can miss the mark dramatically. Imagine putting a charity shop volunteer on some kind of twisted performance-related 'thanks' regime! Whatever technique is used, it must fit.

8. *Initiative fatigue.* I do wonder whether anyone ever actually said that sliced bread was the best thing ever. Certainly citing the 'next best thing' only serves to reinforce cynicism and fatigue. How redesign is talked about is critical to its success, in my view. Presenting it as empowering common sense with a dash of innovation is much more likely to achieve results than describing it as some radical departure from what has always gone on.

9. *Executive commitment.* The senior leaders of any organisation naturally hold the central pillars of how business is done very close to their hearts. Often these same people will have built those pillars in the first place and almost certainly will have been loyal to

them. However, redesign may well require toppling one or more of these pillars. If the leaders balk at this then so will everyone else. The leaders need to understand the critical role that they play in visibly showing their commitment to change.

10. *Multiple accountabilities and demands.* No organisation, no business, operates in a vacuum. Seductive though it is to think only of simple chains of suppliers and customers, it is always more complicated than that. There will be a mixture of regulators, inspectors, the media, competitors, funders, tax authorities, politicians, consumer activists (and so forth) in varying measures. These various people and groups will have different demands and calls on the organisation and its services/products. All these demands need to be understood and at least factored into any redesign, or even harnessed to provide better value for money.

11. *Risk avoidance.* Businesses, business people, staff and directors feel under increasing scrutiny in a world that often appears to be obsessed with finding someone to blame when something goes wrong. Most of us know that when an error occurs or when a service falls very short of what is good practice, it is rarely the fault of a single individual; the causes are more complex and systemic. Nonetheless, this all leads to an atmosphere of caution and various forms of what I call 'back-protection'. This includes not only the simple copying in of all and sundry to emails which say 'not me!' but also the more damaging absence of bold and radical decision-making. This avoidance of risk will corrode attempts to redesign processes and organisations. Praising all innovation, even that which fails, is vital.

There will be other particular hurdles to overcome in your organisation. Always remember that 'culture eats strategy for breakfast'. In other words, changing how an organisation does what it does is never simple or straightforward.

So here are my golden rules of change leadership.

The 20 golden rules of change leadership

1. Have a clear and compelling vision of the future.

2. Form a coalition of the willing, in-touch and influential people to drive the change.

3. Do more communication than you really think is needed (and it still won't be enough).

4. Create discomfort with the current state.

5. Make it safe and OK for people to change, so that no loss of face is experienced.

6. Honour everyone's past achievements and efforts.

7. Identify and tackle what might hinder progress towards the vision.

8. Foster shared learning: encourage people to talk about and challenge the change.

9. Chunk the process into doable steps: a series of hills rather than a big mountain.

10. Know who are the friends and enemies of the change.

11. Channel both enthusiasm and cynicism (cynics are often disappointed enthusiasts).

12. Recognise and thank everyone who is putting in the extra effort, constantly.

13. Ensure the right thinking tools are used in the right places.

14. Look for early wins and talk about them. Lots.

15. Measure progress and results rigorously: qualitatively and quantitatively.

16. Create rituals to help people to deal with the grief that change invokes.

17. Look for ways to symbolise the change.

18. Do more communication than you really think is needed (and it still won't be enough).

19. Network with other leaders who made change happen well; learn from them.

20. Take good care of yourself and others; worthwhile change is never easy.

And yes, I know I repeated item number 3 ...

Now what?

As I said at the beginning, this could have been a much longer book, but this is about the same length as the *Communist Manifesto* by Marx and Engels. Like them, I hope for a revolution. But I want a revolution based on asking good questions, relentlessly, insightfully and optimistically.

I don't mean to be too hard on the legions of transformation consultants who are working diligently for their clients, trying to find ways to improve efficiency and effectiveness. I know how much of a grinding frustration that work can be. But I also know how it could be so different; there are alternative choices to be made by both clients and consultants.

As the world's population grows and demand on our shrinking resources increases, the need for greater productivity (achieving more with less) builds and builds. No doubt technology will help and a combination of 3D printing, nuclear fusion, nanotechnology and genetic research *will* come to be as natural a part of our daily lives as microwaves, smartphones and artesian wells. But we also need greater creativity, elegance and élan in how we do business and provide services. And we need this now. It cannot just wait for the technology.

My hope behind this book was to help you ask the questions that would lead to lasting improvements in productivity. It is a simple revolution.

And it is also my earnest hope that these improvements will be for the benefit of *all*, leading to a fairer world in which *everyone* has opportunity to dream and the resources to achieve those ambitions.

Your own part in this revolution can start here.

Right here.

Right now.

Appendix A: Some further sources of help and ideas

Some questions to stir up some more ideas on how IT might be able to stream-line your business

1. How can your customers/clients/users freely provide you with data (big and small) that helps you understand their needs and requirements more?

2. What information and systems of work can you upload to a cloud in the sky that will overcome geographical separation?

3. How can you create a work system that learns more reliably than people often do?

4. Given the speedy 'searchability' of digital data, what can you now find and find out that hitherto would have taken months of effort?

5. What parts of your business can and should or can and should *not* be automated using IT and other new technology?

6. What mathematical calculations can now be performed that previous circumstances would not allow?

7. How can the immediate transfer of real-time information from one part of your business to another make a difference?

8. From 'one to one' to 'one to many' and now 'many to many', what information can be broadcast and exchanged that could change your business overnight?

9. How might GPS be added to the services you provide to show you where your consumers/users/products are (and have been)?

10. Given the availability of handheld computers, how could you harness the extra control and feedback that you (and your clients etc.) now have?

11. Which is your favourite app/game/website and what could something like it do for your business?

12. What new business/delivery models are now possible?

How to get more from less by shifting from quick-fix to stay-fix approaches to problem solving

1. part one:
https://www.youtube.com/watch?v=RgE3PEmI7yw

2. part two:
https://www.youtube.com/watch?v=Yyp0AQx9meM

Two good books on statistical process control

1. Owen, Mal, and John Morgan. *Statistical Process Control (SPC) in the Office.* Greenfield, 2000

2. Owen, Mal. *SPC and Continuous Improvement.* Springer, 2013

Whole system methods and thinking

1. I have several posts on my blog about this way of approaching change. A good place to start is with this post:
http://jonharveyassociates.blogspot.co.uk/2009/11/making-whole-systems-work.html

2. One of the best books I have come across on this approach to redesigning business and organisations is *Engaging Emergence: Turning Upheaval into Opportunity* by Peggy Holman (Berrett-Koehler, 2010).

3. And the book which began it all for me was *Productive Workplaces: Dignity, Meaning, and Community* (which is now in its third edition for its 25th anniversary) by Marvin R Weisbord (John Wiley & Sons, 2012).

4. Other than these, just search on Open Space (Harrison Owen) or World Café (Juanita Brown) or Future Search (Marvin Weisbord and Sandra Janoff) – there are many resources out there to be used in service of developing a more connected, ambitious, fair and creative world.

Key resources mentioned in the text above

1. Goldratt, Eliyahu M, and Jeff Cox. *The Goal: A Process of Ongoing Improvement.* North River Press, 2014 (now in a 30th anniversary edition)

2. Beckhard, Richard, and Reuben Harris. *Organizational Transitions: Managing Complex Change.* Addison-Wesley, 1977

3. Kipling, Rudyard. 'I Keep Six Honest Serving-Men'. http://www.kiplingsociety.co.uk/poems_serving.htm

4. Hunt-Davis, Ben, and Harriet Beveridge. *Will It Make the Boat Go Faster? Olympic-Winning Strategies for Everyday Success.* Matador, 2011

Leadership in films

There are many, many books about leadership, with several being published every day (see Appendix B, below). Prompted by a Christmas present from my wife, I have been watching lots of films since the end of 2013. After each one, I write a short blog post reviewing the film and highlighting a leadership theme embedded in the movie. You might find these of interest when it comes to *leading* the changes that this book will (hopefully) help you to take: http://jonharveyassociates.blogspot.co.uk/search/label/film

Appendix B: Leadership books and things that have inspired people

A couple of years ago, I began asking a range of people in different places (social media and elsewhere) what book about leadership inspired them. This later turned into not just books about leadership, but any book (or film, or poem, or indeed whatever) which had inspired them to be the leaders that they are.

Many people responded, including some notable celebrities in the shape of Stephen Fry and Alastair Campbell. Below is the list of suggestions from a whole bunch of people from local government, third sector and other public services. There is also a smattering of consultants, several of my colleagues, and some random contacts from Twitter (these are the '@' people below) and elsewhere. I am most grateful to everyone for their suggestions and explanations. Thank you. In many ways, the comments and explanations on why a particular book or film made an impact are the best bits. These may inspire you too.

And watch out for the random repetitions; these could be especially useful books.

Please have a browse and don't be daunted by the fact there are 89 suggestions below. In there could be the book, film or other work that might assist and inspire you to become an even better leader of change.

Item	Recommender	Comment (if any)
21 Irrefutable Laws of Leadership, John C Maxwell	Uzoma Isichei (@Uzomalsichei)	*Almost anything by John Maxwell.*
A Manager's Guide to Leadership, Pedler, Burgoyne and Boydell	Helen Leech, Surrey Library Service	*It's a textbook but I LIKE textbooks. They tell you what to think. This one takes you through 23 'challenges' from developing strategies to making major change. There's a lot of meat in it. Not exactly holiday reading, though.*
A Soldier's Way: An Autobiography, Colin Powell and Joseph E Persico	John-Paul Ruffle, Greater Manchester Police	*A fantastic book on leadership. The key learning points are here: http://govleaders.org/powell.htm*
A Soldier's Way: An Autobiography, Colin Powell and Joseph E Persico	Huw Evans (@wildkippers)	
A Whack on the Side of the Head, Roger von Oech	Gordon Lynn, University of Queensland, Australia	*Full of pearls of wisdom and interesting anecdotes for the aspiring leader but also a few challenges to accepted thinking that may lead to altered leadership practice. Very light, entertaining and thought provoking! Roger has a very good blog site too: http://blog.creative-think.com – quirky, challenging and interesting. He can help you get out of the box ... but it is up to you what you do when you get out!*
Aeneid, Virgil	Lawrence Serewicz, County Durham Council	*Leading refugees into a new country and founding a new country.*
Angels and Ages: A Short Book About Darwin, Lincoln and Modern Life, Adam Gopnik	Nick Keane (@nickkeane)	
Animal Farm, George Orwell	Julie Gibson, Gateshead Council	*Much can be learned from bad practice ;-)*

Item	Recommender	Comment (if any)
Any Given Sunday, Oliver Stone (film)	Lawrence Serewicz, County Durham Council	*Offers an insight into leading a team but at the same time dealing with wider responsibilities.*
As One: Individual Action, Collective Power, Mehrdad Baghai and James Quigley	Graham de Montrose (@montrose77)	*Obviously, as a good corporate citizen, I would recommend As One by Deloitte Global CEO, Jim Quigley.*
Call of the Wild, Jack London	Jessica Rowan, Oxfordshire County Council	*A great adventure story in itself, but a very useful lesson about teams – albeit a team of huskies but still applies. In a harsh and austere environment you can only go forward when you make sure you take care of your team before you take care of yourself.*
Credibility, Kouzes and Posner	Rosie Barfoot, Training for Results	
Credibility, Kouzes and Posner	Marylou Lousvet, Wisework	*I have frequently used the models in the Kouzes and Posner books and the associated leadership profile – though these are textbooks.*
Drive, Daniel Pink	Andy Jones, University of California	*Here are five more books that have taught me a lot.*
Eden, Tim Smit	Louise Reeve, Newcastle City Council	*About the creation of the Eden Project. If ever a team had to overcome any amount of obstacles to create something that had never been done before, it was surely the people involved in building the Eden Project. Very well written and quite amusing in parts!*
Emotional Intelligence, Daniel Goleman	Mike Allen, South Somerset District Council	*Good leadership book.*

Item	Recommender	Comment (if any)
Employee Communication During Mergers and Acquisitions, Jenny Davenport and Simon Barrow	Julia Hines, Age Concern Barnet	*As they say, the soft stuff is the hard part.*
Engaging Emergence: Turning Upheaval into Opportunity, Peggy Holman	Jon Harvey	*Book which sets out the source code for how to tackle wicked problems. A must-read in these austere times in my opinion.*
Genghis Khan and the Making of the Modern World, Jack Weatherford	Vijay Patel, NSPCC	*Definitely an inspired leader – although much maligned.*
Good to Great, Jim Collins	Andy Jones, University of California	*Here are five more books that have taught me a lot*
How to Win Friends and Influence People, Dale Carnegie	Uzoma Isichei (@Uzomalsichei)	*Will make any leader a better one.*
How to Win Friends and Influence People, Dale Carnegie	Steve Keating	*My favourite.*
http://www.knowhownonprofit. org/leadership/role/successful-leadership/gurus	KnowHowNonProfit	*How about some of the books by the leadership gurus?*
http://www.mindtools.com/	Marek Zamborsky, Bedford Council	*Not a book, however bite size structure, manageable, to the point.*
http://www.ted.com/ (video website)	Gordon Lynn, University of Queensland, Australia	*You might also regularly visit TED for some inspiration from a wealth of worldwide presenters. You will be surprised where the inspiration might come from . . .*
http://www.ted.com/talks/ lang/eng/malcolm_gladwell_ on_spaghetti_sauce.html (Malcolm Gladwell, 'Choice, Happiness and Spaghetti Sauce', web video)	Gordon Lynn, University of Queensland, Australia	*My first experience was the marketing of different types of pasta sauce! This was a few years ago but retains its resonance for me even now – something I had never considered. Relevance? It tells you about people and that's who leaders lead.*

Item	Recommender	Comment (if any)
http://www.youtube.com/ watch?v=0pHqw4XZhPE ('Lions Rugby Tour 1997 South Africa – Motivational Speech', web video)	Will Perrin (@willperrin)	*This is good if you don't mind swearing.*
I wouldn't . . .	Carrie Bishop (@carriebish)	*I wouldn't [take leadership inspiration from a book]. I'd find an inspiring role model and learn off them instead.*
Images of Organization, Gareth Morgan	Jacky Hart, Milton Keynes Council	*Looks at organisations using metaphors and challenges how we think about structure and roles.*
In Search of Excellence, Tom Peters and Robert H Waterman Jr	Maurice Griffin, Neath Port Talbot County Borough Council	*The title says it all, really*
Invictus, Clint Eastwood (film)	Bola Odunlami, Essex Police	*I learnt three new things from the characters and scenes: the new president's leadership style, the rugby captain's leadership style and the conversation between the president and the rugby captain.*
Jack: Straight from the Gut, Jack Welch	Rosie Barfoot, Training for Results	*Motivation, given the climate facing the public sector.*
Leadership and the New Science, Margaret J Wheatley	Laura Bennett, North East Lincolnshire Council	*Just brill.*
Leadership: Plain and Simple, Steve Radcliffe	Greg Ockwell, West Sussex County Council	*Straightforward thinking.*
Leading Change, John P Kotter	Simon Misiewicz, Optimise-GB	*If you are looking for change leadership.*
Linchpin, Seth Godin	Dave Briggs, Learning Pool	*Short and to the point.*
Linchpin, Seth Godin	Andy Jones, University of California	*Here are five more books that have taught me a lot.*

Item	Recommender	Comment (if any)
Management of Organizational Behavior, Hersey, Blanchard and Johnson	Jacky Hart, Milton Keynes Council	*These are the books that have inspired or hooked me enough to remember, made me re-examine or want to reread.*
None …	Stephen Fry (@stephenfry)	*None. They're all absolute drivel.*
Not sure …	Matthew Taylor (@RSAMatthew)	*Not sure – I am a bit suspicious of the whole 'leadership' industry to be honest.*
On Leadership, Allan Leighton	Rosie Barfoot, Training for Results	*Inside out leadership.*
Once a Customer, Always a Customer, Chris Daffy	Rod Morphew, BMI Healthcare, Saxon Clinic	
Open Leadership, Charlene Li	Dave Briggs, Learning Pool	*Quite nice.*
Open Leadership, Charlene Li	Ingrid Koeler (@ingridk)	*I will recommend!*
Our Iceberg Is Melting, John Kotter	Simon Misiewicz, Optimise-GB	*Book that would be quite good for training days.*
Patton on Leadership: Strategic Lessons for Corporate Warfare, Alan Axelrod	Steve Wilkinson, North Devon District Council	*Highly recommend.*
Reformation in the House, Tudor Bismark	Uzoma Isichei (@UzomaIsichei)	*For anyone in church leadership, I would strongly recommend [this book].*
Rework, Jason Fried and David Heinemeier Hansson	John Chantler, Planning Advisory Service	*Only takes a couple of hours to read and really makes you want to get stuck in and do.*
Shackleton, Charles Sturridge (film)	Oscar Monteiro, London Borough of Hackney	*http://www.independent.co.uk/ news/uk/home-news/leadership-skills-win-shackleton-belated-acclaim-9217953.html*
South: The Story of Shackleton's Last Expedition 1914–1917, Ernest Shackleton	Oscar Monteiro, London Borough of Hackney	*If you haven't read about Ernest Shackleton, you haven't read about leadership. A cracking Boy's Own story with a textbook example on how to lead people.*

Item	Recommender	Comment (if any)
South: The Story of Shackleton's Last Expedition 1914–1917, Ernest Shackleton	Vijay Patel, NSPCC	*Concur with others on Shackleton*
South: The Story of Shackleton's Last Expedition 1914–1917, Ernest Shackleton	Huw Evans (@wildkippers)	
Spirit Driven Success, Dani Johnson	Uzoma Isichei (@UzomaIsichei)	*Amazing.*
System Failure: Why Governments Must Learn to Think Differently, Jake Chapman	Vijay Patel, NSPCC	*Demos 2004.*
Systems Thinking in the Public Sector, John Seddon	Adrienne Rogers, Dorset County Council	*It turns traditional 'leader' behaviours on their head and challenges the way things are done. A real revelation to anyone who has not come across it before.*
Team of Rivals: The Political Genius of Abraham Lincoln, Doris Kearns Goodwin	Alastair Campbell (@campbellclaret)	*The political genius of Abraham Lincoln.*
The 7 Habits of Highly Effective People, Stephen R Covey	Rosie Barfoot, Training for Results	*Inside out leadership.*
The 7 Habits of Highly Effective People, Stephen R Covey	Simon Misiewicz, Optimise-GB	*Very good.*
The 8th Habit, Stephen R Covey	Rosie Barfoot, Training for Results	*Inside out leadership.*
The Assignment, Mike Murdock	Uzoma Isichei (@UzomaIsichei)	*Extremely good.*
The Diving Bell and the Butterfly, Jean-Dominique Bauby	Louise Reeve, Newcastle City Council	*I'm going to show my age . . . it got me through my A-Levels 11 years ago!*

Item	Recommender	Comment (if any)
The Fifth Discipline, Peter Senge	Rosalind Cannell, Dorset County Council	*Inspires me. [An excerpt:] 'If people imagine their organization as an ocean liner and themselves as the leader, what is their role? For years, the most common answer I received when posing this question to groups of managers was "the captain." Others might say, "The navigator, setting the direction." A few would say "The helmsman, actually controlling the direction," or "the engineer down below stoking the fire, providing energy," or even "the social director . . . " While these are legitimate leadership roles, there is another which, in many ways, eclipses them all in importance. Yet, rarely do people think of it. The neglected leadership role is that of the designer of the ship.'*
The Fifth Discipline, Peter Senge	Dave Briggs, Learning Pool	*Classic.*
The Goal, Eliyahu M Goldratt and Jeff Cox	Jacky Hart, Milton Keynes Council	*Classic novel based approach to management, leadership and its complexity – it's very operational, private sector based.*
The Knowledge: Management and Leadership from A to Z, Carl Taylor	Burning Leaf (@burning_leaf)	
The Leader's Guide to Radical Management, Stephen Denning	Tim Way, Wiltshire Council	
The Leadership Code, Ulrich, Smallwood and Sweetman	Andy Jones, University of California	*Here are five more books that have taught me a lot.*
The Leadership Secrets of Attila the Hun, Wess Roberts	Mike Allen, South Somerset District Council	*Good leadership book.*

Item	Recommender	Comment (if any)
The Little Big Things: 163 Ways to Pursue Excellence, Tom Peters	Andy Jones, University of California	*Here are five more books that have taught me a lot.*
The Living Company: Growth, Learning and Longevity in Business, Arie de Geus	Dave Briggs, Learning Pool	*Classic.*
The New Capitalist Manifesto: Building a Disruptively Better Business, Umair Haque	Tim Way, Wiltshire Council	
The New Polymath, Vinnie Mirchandani	Dave Briggs, Learning Pool	*Pretty good.*
The Prince, Niccolò Machiavelli	Hugh Martyn, Kent County Council	*There is only one book on leadership that is recognised by the top leadership writers in the world as being the seminal thesis on leadership. All my leaders in development are encouraged to read this in order to have legitimacy in their leadership understanding.*
The Richer Way, Julian Richer	Ian Watt, Aberdeen City Council	*Founder of Richer Sounds. It is a short and inexpensive read. It sets out his own vision very clearly on why empowering, and engaging with, staff is the only way to excellent customer satisfaction.*
The Starfish and the Spider, Ori Brafman and Rod A Beckstrom	Peter Ashe, NHS Scotland	*Having been for a long time a bit of a mental refusenik over the element within the paraphernalia of things like competency frameworks, templates for annual personal objectives, etc. that seem to emphasis the individualistic aspects of leader-ship, & having been a fan of networked approaches, influence, etc. . . . I was encouraged to see a book recently about 'the unstoppable power of leaderless organisations'.*

Item	Recommender	Comment (if any)
The Stimulus Factor, David Freemantle	Rosie Barfoot, Training for Results	*Motivation.*
The Tipping Point, Malcolm Gladwell	Jacky Hart, Milton Keynes Council	*These are the books that have inspired or hooked me enough to remember, made me re-examine or want to reread.*
The Worst Journey in the World, Apsley Cherry-Garrard	Solihin Garrard, Makesfive Ltd	*Comment about Shackleton stirs me to recommend. This time it's as much about 'followership' as it is about 'leadership'. It is a superb book by any standards and works on a lot of levels, not the least of which is the role of the goal in judging success, satisfaction and achievement.*
Time to Think: Listening to Ignite the Human Mind, Nancy Kline	Roxanne Persaud (@commutiny)	
Total Leadership: Be a Better Leader, Have a Richer Life, Stewart D Friedman	Helen Foster (@hfos)	*Because it considers leadership in context of whole life, not just professional dimension.*
Touch the Earth: A Self-Portrait of Indian Existence, TC McLuhan	Huw Evans (@wildkippers)	*Jon's suggested book prompted by his suggestion of native American leadership.*
Tribes, Seth Godin	Laura Bennett, North East Lincolnshire Council	*Various stories about getting people on board with a cause/idea and stimulating change – my favourite story is the unicorn in the balloon factory.*
Tribes, Seth Godin	Dave Briggs, Learning Pool	*Short and to the point.*
UnLearning Management: Short Stories on Modern Management, Blair McPherson	Blair McPherson	*As the author I am totally biased, but if you want a different take on management and leadership. To give you a flavor of the book the first chapter is called 'Management isn't what you think it is'.*

Item	Recommender	Comment (if any)
Wave Rider: Leadership for High Performance in a Self-Organizing World, Harrison Owen	Huw Evans (@wildkippers)	
What They Don't Teach You at Harvard Business School, Mark H McCormack	Mike Allen, South Somerset District Council	*Good leadership book.*
Why Leaders Can't Lead: The Unconscious Conspiracy Continues, Warren Bennis	Gerry McMullan, Birmingham City Council	*Nobody seems to have mentioned Warren Bennis. All of his books on leadership are worth reading but the classic is probably [this].*
Xenophon's Cyrus the Great: The Arts of Leadership and War, Larry Hedrick	Ben Donnelly (@brdonnelly)	

Lightning Source UK Ltd.
Milton Keynes UK
UKOW06f0051150316

270209UK00018B/517/P